DATE DUE

JUN 04

Forest

DK

LONDON, NEW YORK, MUNICH,
MELBOURNE, and DELHI

Written and edited by Deborah Lock
and Lorrie Mack
Designed by Janet Allis

Publishing manager Sue Leonard
Managing art editor Clare Shedden
Jacket design Chris Drew
Picture researcher Jo de Gray and
Sarah Stewart-Richardson
Production Shivani Pandey
DTP Designer Almudena Díaz
Consultant Samantha Sawyer

First American Edition, 2004

Published in the United States by DK Publishing, Inc.
375 Hudson Street, New York, New York 10014

04 05 06 07 08 10 9 8 7 6 5 4 3 2 1

Lock, Deborah.
Forest / by Deborah Lock.-- 1st American ed.
p. cm. -- (Eye wonder)
Summary: Introduces characteristics of different kinds of forests
found around the world, the plants and animals that populate them,
and how they are endangered. Includes index.
1. Forest ecology--Juvenile literature. [1. Forest ecology. 2. Forests.
3. Ecology.] I. Title. II Series.
QH541.5.F6L63 2004
577.3--dc22

2003016242
ISBN 0-7894-9893-6 (ALB)—ISBN 0-7894-9759-X (HC)

Color reproduction by Colourscan, Singapore
Printed and bound in Italy by LEGO

Discover more at
www.dk.com

Contents

4-5
Forest features

6-7
Where in the world?

8-9
Tree story

10-11
Awakening forest

12-13
Life in the trees

14-15
Rich pickings

16-17
Falling leaves

18-19
Forest fungi

20-21
Winter journeys

22-23
Needles and cones

24-25
Cold killers

26-27
Frozen forest

28-29
Suffocated forests

30-31
Record-breakers

32-33
Under the canopy

34-35
Rainforest floor

36-37
Getting around

38-39
Up in the clouds

40-41
Dry forests

42-43
Forest fires

44-45
Survival of the forest

46-47
Glossary

48
Index and
acknowledgments

Forest features

Using water, carbon dioxide from the air, and sunlight, leaves produce food for the tree. This process is called photosynthesis.

A large area of trees clumped together is called a forest. However, a forest is much more than this. Step inside and you'll discover a wide variety of plants, with lots of different animals living among them.

Parts of a tree

The trunk of the tree supports the crown of branches, which bear leaves, flowers, fruits, or cones. The roots anchor the tree into the ground and soak up goodness from the soil.

These new leaves shaped like those the fully grown tre

Flowers produce seeds from which new trees can grow.

The bark protects the wood that carries goodness between the branches and the roots.

Birth of a tree

Most seeds are eaten or trampled on, or fall in places where they cannot grow. If a seed survives, its case cracks open. Roots break through, then a stem appears above the ground, and finally the first leaves unfold.

A fallen tree is home to anima such as woodli and millipedes, that feed on th rotting wood.

The roots spread out sideways and downward, soaking up water and minerals.

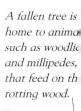

4

A barn owl hunts small animals, such as the shrew.

The forest community

A forest is a massive food web. Parts of living and rotting plants are eaten by many tiny animals, which are eaten by other animals that are hunted by other animals. Changes can affect the balance of the whole community.

A shrew looks for insects to eat.

An oak moth caterpillar eats the leaves of an oak tree.

Where in the world?

autumn · summer · winter · spring

Changing seasons
In some regions, temperature and rainfall change dramatically through the year, so all living things have to adapt. This tree is divided into four sections that show how the branches look in autumn, winter, spring, and summer.

Almost a third of all the land on Earth is covered by trees. I different parts of the world, th climate and the altitude affec the types of trees that can gro There are three main types of forest—deciduous forest, coniferous forest, and rainfore

Find your forest
In cold places, forests are usually coniferou Rainforests grow in hot, damp climates. Areas that are sometimes warm and sometimes cool are called temperate zones. These are where temperate, or deciduous, forests are found.

Coniferous forests

Deciduous forests

NORTH AMERICA

Equator

Rainforests

SOUTH AM

Deciduous forests
Trees that shed their leaves in autumn and grow new ones in spring are known as deciduous. It is never very hot or very cold in these deciduous, or temperate, forests.

Coniferous forests

Where conditions are cool and harsh, trees grow hard, permanent needles for protection instead of leaves that fall off. They also have tough cones in place of flowers to hold their seeds. This type of tree is called coniferous, or evergreen.

Coniferous forests

Deciduous forests

EUROPE

ASIA

AFRICA

Rainforests

Rainforests

AUSTRALIA

Rainforests

Usually found in tropical regions, dense, jungly rainforests grow where the climate is always warm and wet. Although these forests cover only seven percent of the land in the world, more than half of all existing plant and animal species live in them.

7

Tree story

There have been plants of some kind on Earth for 420 million years, but the first forests were full of tall ferns instead of trees. It wasn't until about 210 million years ago that forests began to look like the ones we know today.

Disappearing forests

For thousands of years, people ha depended on trees. At the same time, they have destroyed vast expanses of precious woodland.

Historical rings

Scientists learn a great deal about trees by examining the rings inside their trunks—each ring indicates one year of growth. A wide ring shows that the tree grew quickly that year; a narrow ring means a year when growth was slow.

Robin Hood's Sherwood Forest in England once covered 100,000 acres (405 sq km). Today, it is a 500-acre (2-sq-km) nature reserve.

The outer layer of bark is made up of dead cells that also hold clues to the tree's past life.

Relics of the past

When trees live in damp earth, they are sometimes preserved permanently by minerals in the water. These fossils, called petrified trees, tell us what forest were like millions of years ago.

The oldest wood is at the center of the tree.
It is composed mainly of dead cells.
This old, hard wood is called heartwood.

Changing forests

After the era of ferny plant life, tropical rainforests dominated our planet, which was once warmer than it is now. Later, temperate and evergreen woods spread across lands that were not near the equator.

TOOLS OF DESTRUCTION

Huge areas of early forest were destroyed by the Vikings, a warlike people who lived in northern Europe hundreds of years ago. Vikings thrived because they were good at metalwork, so they could make sharp axes to cut down trees. The wood was used to build houses and ships, then the cleared land was planted with crops.

Dinosaurs roamed freely in prehistoric forests. Stegosaurus, who lived between 206 and 144 million years ago, ate easy-to-reach plant snacks, such as ferns and seed cones.

Awakening forest

Most trees and plants in the deciduous forest come to life in the spring, when the days get longer and the Sun begins to warm the earth. At this time, birds start building nests and baby animals are born.

New life
Even in winter, the trees are dotted with buds. These are covered with hard scales to protect the tiny new flowers, leaves, and stems inside from the cold.

In the light and warmth of the Sun, this horse chestnut bud bursts open.

Wake-up call
Prickly hedgehogs burrow underground when the cold weather comes. They stay there sleeping until springtime, then crawl out and start looking around for food.

Safe home
Huddled safely in a nest made from twigs and leaves, these bullfinch chicks are being fed by their father. His bright pink chest makes him easy to identify.

abe in the woods

ed deer live mostly in wooded
aces. Their young have
otted coats that blend
to the speckled light
tering through the trees.
his camouflage makes it
rder for predators to find them.

Flowering forest

Before the tall trees get
covered with leaves, lots
of sun can get through, so
bluebells, foxgloves, and
other wild flowers carpet
the forest in springtime.

Life in the trees

A single tree in a forest can be a home, a food source, or a shelter for a variety of animals. Often hidden from view, there is a world of wildlife activity.

The gray squirrel uses its bushy tail to balance as it runs around, and twitches it to communicate with other squirrels.

Tree-dwellers

High up in the trees, squirrels' nests, called drays, can be found hidden among the branches. After scurrying down to the ground to find fruits and stored nuts, squirrels return there to rest.

Insect farmers

Aphids feed on the sap of plants. They produce a sticky liquid called honeydew that ants eat. Often ants can be seen rubbing the aphids to squeeze out the honeydew. In return,

After using its pointed beak to peck through the bark, a green woodpecker can reach into the tree with its long, sticky tongue to lick up any hidden insect larvae.

plant that uses a tree as a support to climb up toward the sunlight.

Burrowers

The tangled web of a tree's roots provides an ideal place for badgers to dig out their home, called a sett. Usually, this has a number of entrance holes and sleeping chambers with underground tunnels linking them together.

Forest facts

- Green woodpeckers prefer ants and can eat 2,000 a day.

- When badgers leave their setts, foxes or rabbits often come to live there.

- Some beetles lay their eggs within the bark of a tree. When the larvae hatch out, they are near their food.

Rich pickings

Forest plants and animals help each other. For example, some animals eat berries and nuts, while others help to fertilize plants by taking pollen from one flower to another. Sometimes, animals carry seeds to where they have plenty of space, light, and food to grow.

Sweet nectar

When insects land on flowers to drink the nectar, powdery pollen sticks to their legs and bodies. As they move on, the pollen goes with them to fertilize the next flower.

Pollen clings to bees' fuzzy bodies.

Fruity flowers

Once they've been fertilized, flowers turn into fruit or nuts. These contain the seeds that will become new plants.

Forest facts

● Most fleshy fruits, such as berries, contain lots of seeds. Nuts are hard, dry fruits with just one seed inside.

● Each seed has a baby plan and a supply of food enclosed inside a hard case.

● Flowers have bright petals and strong, sweet scents to attract insects.

Nutty name

Nuthatches get their name from the nuts they eat. They have very strong beaks so they can get inside tough shells easily.

Buried treasure
Chipmunks bury acorns in the earth, so they'll have food for the winter. Often, they forget what they've done, and the acorns grow into oak trees!

Hitching a ride
Some seeds are stored inside sticky burs that get caught on animal fur. Eventually, they fall off, and some of them land on fertile ground.

Feasting for winter
This American black bear is filling up on woodland berries. During the autumn, he needs to eat as much as he can to keep him going through the long, cold winter.

Falling leaves

In the autumn, the forest floor becomes littered with the multicolored leaves that have fallen off the trees. Many creepy-crawlies feed on the rotting leaves, while other animals feast on these tiny animals.

Color changes

Leaves get their color from green chlorophyll, which absorbs the energy in sunlight. When the tree uses up all the chlorophyll, its leaves turn yellow and red.

Hide and seek

Hidden among the thick layers of rotting leaves, the woodcock uses its long bill to poke around for tiny animals to eat. With eyes positioned high on its head, it keeps a lookout for enemies at the same time.

Sticky tongue

At night, toads waddle from their dark shelters in search of insects, larvae, spiders, slugs, and worms to catch on their sticky tongues.

Snails have rough tongues to break off their food.

Insects make up 70 percent of the animals in a deciduous forest.

...ped forager

...striped skunk uses its long, sharp
...s to dig into burrows and rotting
...d for all sorts of food. If threatened,
it aims a foul-smelling
spray at its enemy.

A bed for the winter

During the autumn, the dormouse
feasts on hazelnuts. As the weather
becomes colder, it makes a nest of
leaves and grass, then curls up to
sleep until spring.

Soil from inside the tunnels gets piled up into molehills.

Underground tunnels

As the mole moves quickly through its
maze of underground tunnels, it eats
the earthworms and other animals
that have fallen inside.

Forest fungi

Fungi play a vital role in a forest. They feed on dead plants and animals, turning them into nutrients, which enrich the soil. Then other plants soak up these nutrient to stay healthy.

The bright red co warns that this fu is poisonous.

Puff, puff!

To distribute its spores, the puffball puffs them out of a hole in its cap, like a cloud of smoke. The many millions of spores are then carried away by the wind.

Under the cap are the gills, which is where the spores are stored.

Partners

Some fungi, such as fly agaric, form a partnership with a tree nearby. They link up with the tree's roots and supply it with nutrients. The tree gives them moisture and food.

In the soil is the main part of the fungus—a maze of thin threads searching for food.

eadly taste

e mushroom cap
d stalk are the only
rts of a fungus that
n be seen. For people,
e death cap is one
the most poisonous
shrooms in the world.

*The stalk base shows the
remains of a veil that
once protected the cap.*

*As it grows, the cap
is joined to the stalk
before it opens out.*

*The bracket-shaped
cap of the birch
polypore becomes
flatter and darker
as it gets older.*

The parasites

Often, a group of
birch polypores
attack a living birch
tree, feeding on it and
draining it of its food
supplies. Eventually
they kill the tree and
then continue to live
there feeding on the
dead wood.

autumn, the mushroom, or fruit, of the fungus appears.

Forest words

Nutrients These are the
minerals and other useful
substances that plants need
for growth and strength.

Parasite Something that
feeds off another living thing.

Spores These are the tiny
seeds of a fungus.

19

Winter journeys

Every year, almost half of all the world's birds travel from the forest where they breed in the summer to a warmer climate where they can feed in the winter. These flights, known as migration, are often long and dangerous, and they use up a huge amount of energy.

Spot the birdie

This spotted flycatcher is showing how it got its name. Some of its relatives spend their summers in Europe, then fly to Africa in the autumn. Others breed in North America, and travel to Central or South America for the winter.

Moving on

Honey buzzards (see below) are large birds that feed on the meat they get from hunting. They breed in the forests of Great Britain, but when winter comes, they fly to Africa.

EUROPE

ASIA

AFRICA

Honey buzzard migration route

Coming home

Baby honey buzzards like to eat wasp larvae. There are lots of these in British forests in May, so this is the time when the adults return from Africa to breed.

These babies grow up fa

Living the high life

Orioles spend most of their lives high up in the trees. Once in a while, they sweep down to the ground to splash in a lake or a pond, or to pick up nuts and insects to eat.

Golden orioles usually winter in Africa, but this one has left its European home to soak up the sun in Oman, near the Arabian Sea.

Spreading their wings

In September, the honey buzzard sets off again for Africa. These birds are adapted to flying long distances by having big wings and a long tail.

they'll be able to fly south with their parents.

Travel options

Blue jays are found all across North America, as far south as Texas. Some of them fly south in winter, but others stay where they are, storing food, such as nuts and acorns, to last them through the colder weather.

Migrating facts

● Arctic terns travel 21,000 miles (35,000 km) every year, from the Arctic to the Antarctic and back again.

● Before they set off, some small birds eat enough to double their weight. This extra fat gives them energy for their long journey.

Needles and cones

Forests in chilly climates are full of Christmas trees, such as pines, spruces, and firs. Instead of papery leaves that drop off in the autumn, they have hard needles that stay on all year long. These trees are known as evergreens.

Male moose have huge antlers with up to 20 points on each one.

Giant deer

The largest member of the deer family— the moose—lives in coniferous forests. In the winter, it munches on tree bark, and sometimes eats so much from one tree that the tree dies.

Spiky rodent

The slow-moving porcupine can be found noisily chewing leaves and branches in trees, or on the forest floor. It can raise its many thousands of spiky quills when threatened.

Capercaillies are about the size of turkeys.

Dancing display

In the spring, male capercaillies gather together and perform a dance to attract a female. They make a drum-roll, gurgling sound and leap around.

Forest facts

● The dark green needles stay on so that they can start making food for the tree as soon as the weather warms up.

● In dry weather, the scales on the cones open out and the seeds fall out.

● Little sunlight gets through the trees, so only small plants grow on the dark forest floor.

rd case

e this hardy spruce, most needle-
 trees produce scaly cones that
tect their seeds. This kind of
 is called a conifer.

Antlers are covered with smooth, furry skin that is known as "velvet."

Cold killers

Hunting for food is a challenge in the cold, dark forests. The hungry predators have to cover large territories to find enough to eat. They have adopted fierce and clever techniques to track down and kill their prey.

Wolf facts

- Wolves are the largest members of the dog family.

- A wolf pack is led by a main male and his mate. This pair always eats from the prey first.

- A wolf pack eats almost every part of a carcass because they never know when their next big meal will be.

Pack hunters

Gray wolves work as a team to catch large animals, such as moose and caribo Through scent, sound, and sight, they search for a weak animal. They then split into smaller groups to surround it and, when close enough they all break in a run to catch

Air attack

The long-eared owl glides and hovers almost silently, searching for small animals and birds to catch. It gets its name from the two tufts of feathers on its head, which are not ears at all.

Agile raider

Always hungry, the pine marten hunts for any small animal on the woodland floor, and has the agility to climb trees for raiding nests and catching tree-dwellers. Nuts and fruits are also part of its varied diet.

...e glutton

...e ferocious wolverine is named the ...utton" due to its very large appetite. ...hough it's only the size of a small dog, ...hases reindeer into snowdrifts and kills ...m with a bite from its powerful jaws.

Frozen forest

During winter in the coniferous forests, the temperature can drop to below −40°C. The ground is frozen hard and covered with snow. With very few hours of daylight, how do the plants and wildlife survive?

The waxy-co[...]
needles and
the downwar[...]
slanting bran[...]
let the snow s[...]
off without
breaking ther[...]

Forest retreat
In the winter, caribou move into forested areas to find food. They scrape the snow with their broad hooves to uncover the lichen.

Fur coat

Living only in the cold land of Siberia, the sable has thick fur to keep itself warm. However, people nearly hunted the sable to extinction for its coat.

arp-eyed

th sharp eyesight, the
thern goshawk perches
branches to watch for
bird or animal to catch.
rounded wings and long
allow it to fly swiftly between
trees. The goshawk moves from
territory when food is scarce.

The big sleep

Just before winter, black bears eat lots of food so they put on a thick layer of body fat. Then they find a cave, or den, where they can sleep during the very cold months. During this time, when food is not available, they can live off their fat.

ARCTIC TRAVELERS

Reindeer" is the name given to tame
aribou that are owned by people
ving in the Arctic. The reindeer can
e ridden, or used to pull sleds. Some
re eaten and their hides are used for
lothing. At the end of the winter, the
erds leave the forests and head north
r the summer. They can walk easily
on the snow because
their broad hooves
spread out, acting
like snowshoes.
The people pack
up and travel
with them.

27

Suffocated forests

Large areas of conifer forests in Europe and North America are dying. Many scientists believe this is because air pollution coming from thousands of miles away is damaging the trees.

Burning fuels

Factories, power stations, and cars are all involved in the burning of gasoline, oil, or coal. Whenever this happens, chemicals, such as sulfur and nitrogen, are released into the air.

Clouds are then swept over long distance

Action box

What can we do to help?

● Use less electricity by turning off lights, computers, and other electrical appliances when we are not using them.

● Only fill a teakettle with the amount of water we need. Boiling a full kettle uses up more gas or electricity.

● Use a car less by walking, cycling, sharing car trips, and using public transportation.

Acid mix

Inside clouds, the chemicals mix with water vapor and turn into acid. The clouds sweep across to the forests. Then the acids fall in rain or snow, damaging the tree

Liming the lakes
Animals and plants living in the lakes and rivers are killed by the acids. By pouring lime into the water, the lakes become less poisonous, so that fish and plants can survive.

d attack
ls damage the needles, so the
s cannot produce enough food
ay healthy. Pests and diseases
now attack more easily.

Poisoned trees
Acids also soak into the soil. Trees cannot grow well in the poisonous soil and eventually die. Even if air pollution is reduced dramatically, it would take many years for the damaged forests to recover.

the coniferous forests by air currents.

Record-breakers

Plants hold the records for being the world's biggest and oldest living things. Ancestors from one particular species have lived on Earth for over 150 million years. How have they achieved this?

Oldest living trees

On the dry, barren slopes of the White Mountains of California, free from competition from other trees, are the aged bristlecone pines. One, named "Methuselah," is 4,768 years old, and was a seedling when the Egyptian

The ginkgo family of trees grows throughout the world, and has survived for millions of years due to its resistance to disease and pests.

General Sherman

The largest living thing (by volume) is a giant sequoia tree named "General Sherman." It has a very, very thick trunk. Its total mass is estimated to be ten times more than a blue whale, and it is still growing!

Drive-through

The towering redwoods thrive on the damp, rich soils of the Californian coastal forests. The tallest one is 365 ft (111.25 m) tall, which is about the size of an Apollo space rocket.

Under the canopy

From above, rainforests appear as a vast green canopy, such as in the Amazon. Underneath, plants are growing everywhere These forests are an amazing, colorful, and noisy home for a wide variety of animals.

Jewel of the forest

Light on the wings of the blue morpho reflects a stunning blue color. But the wings' underside is brown with eyespots, which makes the butterfly hard to see when it rests.

Twisting arou
the tall tree t
and branches
fast-growing
called lianas.

Thick, ropelike creepers grow upward toward the light.

Slow and steady

Moving slowly, the unusual two-toed sloth hangs upside-down from branches with its hooklike claws. Its damp fur is covered by algae and filled with insects.

Terror of the forest

Watching eagle-eyed from a look-out branch, the harpy eagle is the biggest and strongest bird in the rainforest. Its large gripping talons can pull a sloth out of a tree.

Flashes of color

In the canopy, colorful
scarlet macaws fly around,
filling the forests with
screeching calls.
They are only silent
when eating.

e pools inside
bromeliads are
ne to more
n 250 different
mals, such as
js and insects.

Air plants

Rooted in tree
nks, high above
e ground, bromeliads
urish. Rainwater
llects in the center,
d this provides a drink
r many animals.

33

Rainforest floor

Plants with large, shiny leaves, scented flowers, and tasty fruits, as well as dead leaves falling from the branches of trees high above, cover the ground in a rainforest. It's a busy place with much of the action hidden from our sight.

Buttress roots

A tangle of far-reaching roots spread out across the rainforest floor. The soil is thin and does not have much goodness, so the roots grow out from the trunks to support the tall trees and soak up much-needed nutrients near the soil's surface.

Ant-eaters

A tamandua uses its sharp front claws to open up ant nests, and then puts a long, sticky tongue inside to lick up the ants. It does not destroy the nests, so that it can return another time.

Pollinator

Feeding at night, the fast-flying long-tongued bat visits strongly scented flowers. The flower's pollen falls onto the bat and gets passed to the next flower the bat visits.

g squeeze

rled up in low branches, the world's heaviest ke, the anaconda, rests for days after a je meal. It kills by wrapping its powerful ly around its prey and squeezing until animal can't breathe. Anacondas llow their victims whole, headfirst.

This bat has a long, narrow tongue to drink the nectar inside the flower.

Nighttime meals

Scampering along a system of paths, this paca (a small rodent) sniffs out fruits and leaf buds in the dark. Pacas shelter in burrows or hollow trees during the day.

Leaf-cutters

Busy leaf-cutter ants cut out pieces of leaves and carry them over their heads to their underground nests. The fungus that grows on the chewed leaves is food for the ants.

WORLD'S STRONGEST

Rainforests are home to over 30 million species of insects. Some insects, such as the rhinoceros beetle, play a very important part in recycling the nutrients in rotting wood and leaves back into the soil for use by living plants. While humans can carry only about three times their body weight, rhinoceros beetles can carry an amazing 850 times their own weight. They get their name from the horn on their head, which they use for fighting rivals, digging, and climbing.

Getting around

The dense rainforests are like large adventure playgrounds with so many plants for climbing up, scrambling over, swinging across, or jumping from. But the animals are not necessarily playing.

Leaping lemurs

Lemurs can leap from tree to tree to escape from enemies. They hold their bodies upright as they jump so that their hands and feet are ready to grip the next tree trunk.

Lemurs use their powerful hind legs to spring from trees.

Prowlers

The jaguar's spotted coat breaks up its outline among the plants on the forest floor. Camouflaged, it quietly prowls around searching for animals to eat. It can even climb low branches to catch monkeys.

Cautious climber

At night, the slow-moving pottos awake to search for foo trying to avoid being se by predators. It places one strong gripping foot in front of anoth as if walking on a tightrope.

Swingers

In the forests of Borneo and North Sumatra, orangutans can be found living in the trees. Their very long arms, which span up to 8 ft (2.5 m), are ideal for swinging from branch to branch.

liders

...ctive at night, the colugo
...s a thin, furry layer of skin
...etching from its fingers
... its tail. It spreads
...s out as it glides
...om tree to tree
... search of
...nts to eat.

...ng orangutans
... with their
...thers for up to
... years, learning
... them.

Up in the clouds

Most tropical rainforests lie in low places, such as river valleys. However, some of them grow so high up on mountains that they are in the middle of a cloud all the time. This special damp environment is home to lots of rare animals and plants.

Mountain monkey

Pileated gibbons are small apes that live in the Cardamom Mountain forests of Thailand. Bit by bit, the trees are being cleared, so the gibbons face extinction.

Nosy neighbor

At home in New Guinea's mountain forests, the long beaked echidna is one of the few mammals that lay eggs. The nose that gives this creature its name can be up to 8 in (20 cm) long.

Living together

The cloud forest of Malaysia is one of the last sites in the world where Asian elephants, rhinos, and tigers all live in the same place. Asian elephants have much smaller ears than their African cousins.

Brilliant plumage

Gripping a branch with its small feet, this resplendent quetzal displays its shimmering colors high up in the branches of the Costa Rican cloud forest. Only the male birds have these exotic feathers.

Gorillas in the mist

The cloud forest of central Africa is one of the few places mountain gorillas are found. Conservationists work hard to keep their habitat safe and protect them from hunters.

NATURE'S NURSERY

Many of the plants that grow in cloud forests cannot be found anywhere else. In the mountain forests of Peru, for example, there are thought to be more than 1,000 species of rare orchids. One small area alone contains more different types of plant than are found on the whole continent of Europe.

Dry forests

Not many plants can survive the hot, dry Australian summers, but fast-growing eucalyptus trees flourish. Among them live many marsupials—animals with pouches where their babies live when they are first born.

Peck, peck!

Although long-billed corellas nest in the hollows of eucalyptus trees, they feed on the ground. Pecking with their pointed bills, they search for bulbs, seeds, and fruits to eat.

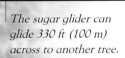

The sugar glider can glide 330 ft (100 m) across to another tree.

Sweet tooth

A sugar glider has a thin layer of skin between its fingers and its ankles. It spreads th out when it wants to glide to another tree ir search of sweet things to eat, such as the gur and sap from the trees

Many flowers have no petals and only the stamens show.

Gripping tails

As pygmy possums feed on the pollen and nectar from sweet-scented flowers, they cling on using their long, gripping tails. They are the smallest marsupials.

Banded anteater

Like anteaters, numbats have a long snout to sniff out ants' nests, sharp front claws to dig them out, and a long, sticky tongue for licking up the ants. They shelter inside hollow logs.

The evergreen eucalyptus leaves have a tough coating that stops water loss.

Little devil

Tasmanian devils are so named because they have a loud screech and fierce looks, and now live only in Tasmania. Their favorite food is dead animals.

"No drink"

Koala is an Aboriginal word meaning "no drink." The cuddly-looking koala feeds entirely on eucalyptus leaves and gets enough water from them. Often it spends 80 percent of its day asleep.

Waratah

The large, dome-shaped flowerheads of the waratah shrub are made up of hundreds of small flowers. The bright colors attract birds to feed on the nectar the flower produces.

Forest fires

Fires can help forests to recycle goodness in dead plants and to clear the way for new growth. However, if a forest fire gets out of control, it can cause lots of damage.

Fighting fires

On the ground, firefighters try to stop the fire from spreading. They cut down trees to make a gap called a firebreak.

Goggles keep sparks out of firefighters' eyes.

Fireproof clothing protects the firefighters from the heat.

Axes and chainsaws are used to cut down trees.

Raining buckets

Helicopters dip large buckets into nearby lakes to scoop up large amounts of water, which are then released over the fire. Within minutes, the helicopters can be back with another load.

Florida

Smoke from forest fires

Lake Monroe

ooling the fire

efighting planes called airtankers are used to
ur thousands of gallons of fire retardant over
flames. The retardant is a red-dyed liquid,
ich slows down and cools a fire.

Fire watch

Space satellites can help firefighters by
producing infrared pictures of big blazes.
On this one, which shows part of the
state of Florida, smoke is blue, plants are
red, ground is green or brown, buildings
are blue or gray, and water is black.

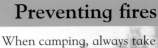

me fir trees need a fire's heat to release their seeds.

Preventing fires

When camping, always take
extra care when using fire, by

● storing flammable liquid
containers in a safe place,

● never taking burning
sticks out of a fire,

● always making sure the
campfire is out when leaving.

New life

In among the burned remains
of a forest, new seedlings soon
appear. They grow quickly
with little competition, more
sunlight, and renewed
goodness in the soil.

Survival of the forest

All over the world, forests are being destroyed. Some trees are cut down for their wood, but often it's their land that is wanted for farms, buildings, or industry. In some places, though, disappearing forests are slowly being replaced.

Cultivation

The Brazilian rainforest is one of the world's most famous endangered habitats. Here, a large chunk of it has been cleared to provide commercial farmland.

Giant problem

Over the last few decades, the Chinese forest habitat of the giant panda has shrunk by 50 percent. Threatened with extinction, this creature has become a world symbol of conservation.

LAST-MINUTE SAVE

Butterflies of all kinds are threatened b the destruction of their forest habitat. During the 20th century, for example, the numbers of Schaus swallowtail butterflies in Florida fell so low that they nearly became extinct.

To save them, a large conservation program was launched, and today their population is growing and thriving.

Taking care

Once new trees are planted, trained conservationists keep watch to make sure they are growing normally, and that they stay free from pests and diseases.

Damage repair

To replace forests destroyed years ago, these Sri Lankan children are planting tree seedlings they have grown themselves on the hills near their village.

ew for old

me forests are designed
 be replanted as soon as
ey are cut down. These
 known as sustainable
 ests. Here, new seedlings
 e well protected so they
 n grow as tall as the
 es around them.

Forests are very
precious—find a
tree to love
today!

How can I help?

Paper is made from trees, so try not to waste it, and recycle as much as you can to help keep our future forests safe.

Glossary

Here are the meanings of some words it is useful to know when you are learning about trees and forests.

Acorn the smooth, hard fruit of the oak tree.

Algae simple plants without roots, stems, or leaves, which usually grow in water.

Bark tough protective layer on the outside of a tree's trunk and branches.

Bromeliad a type of epiphyte that has a rosette of stiff leaves at the top where rainwater collects.

Bud small bump that turns into a flower, a leaf, or a stem.

Bur a fruit or seed with a prickly or sticky covering.

Buttress root a root that grows from a stem or trunk, near the soil's surface.

Carbon dioxide colorless gas absorbed from the atmosphere by plants.

Camouflage color or pattern that helps a plant or animal blend into its surroundings.

Chlorophyll the green chemical in plants that uses the Sun's warmth and light.

Climate the average weather of an area in terms of rain, wind, temperature, and so on.

Cone the fruit of a coniferous tree. Cones have scales on the outside to protect their seeds.

Coniferous having cones to hold seeds instead of flowers and fruits. Coniferous trees have needles instead of leaves.

Conservation the process of saving plants and animals from damage and destruction.

Deciduous having leaves that drop off in autumn, and grow again in spring.

Diet the food and liquid tha a particular animal eats.

Dray squirrel's nest. Drays, which are the size of a socce ball, are lined with leaves.

Epiphyte a plant that grows on another plant, but does not use its food or water.

Evergreen having permane leaves or needles.

Extinct plant or animal species that has died out.

Fern simple plant; one of th first to grow on Earth.

Fertile (soil) rich in the nutrients plants need to grow

Firebreak strip of bare land intended to stop a fire.

wer the part of a plant
ponsible for reproduction.

uit the part of a plant that
ntains its seeds.

hens low-growing plants
nd on hard surfaces like
ks, trees, and bare ground.

gration moving from one
ce to another to find food
warmth.

ctar sweet liquid inside
wers that attracts insects.

edles long, hard, needle-
ped leaves usually found
conifer trees.

t hard, dry fruit with one
ge seed inside.

trients "foods" that plants
d animals need to stay
lthy.

asite plant or animal that
es its nutrients from
other living thing.

rified (trees)
served by minerals
olved in water.

otosynthesis the
y plants use water,
bon dioxide, and
light to produce
d.

len powder
duced by
vers for use in
roduction.

Pollution harmful gases and
particles in the air.

Predator an animal that kills
other animals for food.

Prey an animal hunted by
other animals for food.

Rainforest dense forest that
grows in hot, wet climates.

Root the part of a plant that
absorbs and stores food and
water from the earth.

Seed case containing the tiny
beginnings of a new plant,
and enough food to help it
start growing.

Seedling young plant that
has grown from a seed.

Sett badger's
underground
home, or
burrow.

Species group of living things
that have characteristics in
common, and can breed with
one another.

Spore tough case containing
a tiny collection of cells that
can produce a new plant.

Sustainable (forest) designed
to be replanted when it is cut.

Temperate a climate that is
never very hot or very cold.

Tropics the hot regions on
either side of the equator.

Trunk the main stem of a
tree, which supports its roots
and branches.

Index

anaconda 35
ants 12, 34, 35, 40
aphids 12
Arctic tern 21

badger 13
barn owl 5
beetle 13, 35
birch tree 19
black bear 15, 27
blue jay 21
blue morpho butterfly 32
bristlecone pine tree 30
bromeliads 33
bullfinch 10
buttress roots 34

camouflage 11, 36
capercaillie 22
caribou *see* reindeer
chipmunk 15
colugo 37
coniferous forests 6-7, 22-29
conservation 39, 44-45

deciduous forests 6, 10-19
dormouse 17

echidna 38
elephant 38
eucalyptus tree 40, 41
extinction 27, 38, 44

fire 42-43
food web 5

fungi 18-19

giant panda 44
giant sequoia tree 31
gibbon 38
ginkgo tree 30
gorilla 39
gray wolf 24
green woodpecker 13

harpy eagle 32
hedgehog 10
honey buzzard 20-21
horse chestnut tree 10

insects 5, 14, 16, 21, 32, 33, 35
ivy 13

jaguar 36

koala 41

leaf-cutter ants 35

lemur 36
lianas 32
long-billed corella 40
long-eared owl 25
long-tongued bat 35

migration 20
mole 17
moose 22-23

northern goshawk 27
numbat 40
nuthatch 14

oak moth caterpillar 5
oak tree 5, 15
orangutan 37
orchid 39
oriole 21

paca 35
petrified trees 8
photosynthesis 4

pine marten 25
pollution 28-29
porcupine 22
potto 36
pygmy possum 40

rainforests 6-7, 9, 32-39, 44
red deer 11
redwood tree 31
reindeer 25, 26, 27
resplendent quetzal 3
rhino 38
rhinoceros beetle 35

sable 27
scarlet macaw 33
Schaus swallowtail butterfly 44
shrew 5
snail 16
spotted flycatcher 20
squirrel 12
striped skunk 17
sugar glider 40

tamandua 34
Tasmanian devil 41
tiger 38
toad 16
tree rings 8
two-toed sloth 32

waratah 41
wolverine 25
woodcock 16

Acknowledgments

Dorling Kindersley would like to thank:
Janet Allis for original illustrations; Sarah Mills and Gemma Woodward for picture library services; Jacqueline Gooden and Laura Roberts for design assistance.

Picture credits

The publisher would like to thank the following for their kind permission to reproduce their photographs:
a=above; c=center; b=below; l=left; r=right; t=top;

Alamy Images: Jim Nicholson 8cr; Alan Wheeler 41background, **Ardea London Ltd:** 36cl; Ian Beams 17tr; Jean-Paul Ferrero 40crb, 44bl; Masahiro Iijima 27tr; Jaime Plaza Van Roon 41br, **Bruce Coleman Ltd:** Bruce Coleman Inc 32-33; Marie Read 21bl; **Corbis:** Chris Beddall/Papilio 17br; Niall Benvie 11; D Boone 42bl; Andrew Brown 10tl; Andrew Brown/Ecoscene 6clb; Mike Buxton/Papilio 14bc; Gary W Carter 15tl; Ralph A Clevenger, W Cody 7tl, 22cla;W Perry Conway 10cl, 15bc, 27tl; D Robert & Lorri Franz 24bl; Michael and Patricia Fogden 38-39; Gaetano 45tl; Raymond Gehman 42bc; Collart Herve/Sygma 35tl; Dave G Houser 43bc; Wolfgang Kaehler 35br; Galen Rowell 30bc; Gary Joe McDonald 7tc, 24bc; Gunter Marx

Photography 23cla; Massimo/Mastrorillo 28tl; Robert Y Ono 22bc; Michael Pole J M Roberts 42cb; Sanford/Angliolo 2br; Walter Schmid 6cla; Kennan Ward 39 Randy Wells 46-47; Tony Wharton,/FLPA 19tr; Terry Whittaker/FLPA 35clb, **D Picture Library:** 16bc; Brian Cosgrove 28-29; Natural History Museum 5crb, 6cl 14ca; Richmond Park; Alan Watson 7cr; Jerry Young 7cr, 6bl, **FLPA - Images c nature:** Frans Lanting 44ca, **Nature Picture Library Ltd:** Martin Dohn 28bc; H and Jens Eriksen 21tr; Jeff Foott 8crb; Jorma Luhta 22bl; Dietmar Nill 24-25, 35 Premaphotos 12bc; Jeremy Walker 8tl, **N.H.P.A.:** ANT 40ca; G I Bernard 45clb Stephen Dalton 18tl; Manfred Daneggar 25cr; J Dennis 36ca; Martin Harvey 38 Daniel Heuclin 36bc; Robert Erwin 15tr; Pavel German 38cra; T Kitchen & V F 17cla, 25cl; Mike Lane 42tr; Eero Murtomaici 20bc; Dr Ivan Polunin 37tl; Andy Rouse 13cla, 36-37; Jany Sauvanet 32br; Kevin Schafer 39tr; Roger Tidman 17c WLD 33cla, **Oxford Scientific Films:** ER Degginger/AA 12cla; Breck Kent 30-Stan Osolinski 38clb; Richard Packwood 29bc; Alan Root 34bc; **Popperfoto:** 43 **Lynn Rogers:** 1, 27bc; **RSPB Images:** Paul Doherty 21c, **Science Photo Librar** Earth Satellite Corporation 43tr, **Still Pictures:** Mark Edwards 29tr, 45tr; Klien/Hubert 41tl; Dani/Jeske 31bc; Bruno Pambour 29tl; Roland Seitre 33br; Je Claude Teyssier 10cr; **Getty Images:** Laurie Campbell 13crb; Angelo Cavalli 18 Daniel J Cox 26; Howie Garber 40tl; Kevin Schafer 34; Gary Randall 12-13; Lo Adamski-Peek 45br.

All other images © Dorling Kindersley
For further information see: www.dkimages.com